John Wesley Powell
and the
Mighty Colorado

SO-BED-956

by Alexandra Ericson
illustrated by Jeffrey Thompson

Harcourt
SCHOOL PUBLISHERS

Requests for permission to make copies of any part of the work should be addressed to School Permissions and Copyrights, Harcourt, Inc., 6277 Sea Harbor Drive, Orlando, Florida 32887-6777. Fax: 407-345-2418.

HARCOURT and the Harcourt Logo are trademarks of Harcourt, Inc., registered in the United States of America and/or other jurisdictions.

Printed in China

ISBN 10: 0-15-350990-2
ISBN 13: 978-0-15-350990-2

Ordering Options
ISBN 10: 0-15-350601-6 (Grade 4 On-Level Collection)
ISBN 13: 978-0-15-350601-7 (Grade 4 On-Level Collection)
ISBN 10: 0-15-357943-9 (package of 5)
ISBN 13: 978-0-15-357943-1 (package of 5)

4 5 6 7 8 9 10 0940 12 11 10 09

Slowly and carefully, Major John Wesley Powell checked and rechecked the supplies. It was May of 1869. On this day, he and nine men would begin a journey that no person had ever taken. Their adventure would begin in Green River in what is now Wyoming. Their goal was to ride down the mighty Colorado River.

Major Powell stepped into his boat, the *Emma Dean*, which was named after his wife. Three other boats would hold the rest of the group. "Run up the flags now and shove off!" shouted Major Powell. With that, the men pushed the boats off into the waters, and the journey had begun!

No one had ever taken a trip down the Colorado because the rapids were so dangerous. Major Powell had been warned repeatedly about these dangers, but he was determined to make the trip.

It was not the first time Powell would face danger. He had fought bravely in the Civil War and had lost his arm doing so. Major Powell was also a scientist and an explorer. His interest in nature made him want to explore. Now he would explore the Colorado River.

The water was fast and deep as it swirled around the boats. Soon the tiny town of Green River and the people watching from the riverbanks faded into the distance.

Major Powell and his party were now completely on their own. There would be almost no cities or towns along the way. So, they would have to use the supplies they brought with them or hunt for food. It was not the first time the men in Powell's party had to live off of the land. Most were mountain men who had faced danger before. But even so, the party of ten had no idea what lay ahead.

During the first few weeks of the trip, the boats flowed along the Green River. The Green River meets up with the Colorado River. The Green River wound through the pink desert lands of what is now Utah. Powell was a good leader. He often sang songs while the men rowed. The men sang too, their voices rising above the roar of the rushing waters.

Each night, Powell made careful notes in his diary. The landscape was magnificent. The stepped buttes of the land were a rich red. But in the setting sun they were hues of pinks, blues, and yellows. Looking out over the sunset, Powell felt that this would be a memorable trip indeed.

As the boats moved along the Green River, the landscape changed. Mountain sheep grazed along the steep sides of the canyons. In the background, herds of elk could be seen in open, grassy land.

Parts of the trip were through water that was smooth and gentle. At other times, the men endured swift, moving waters that threatened to overturn the boats. Rocks sticking up out of the water were also a danger. One wrong move and a boat could crash against a rock, its contents spilling out into the river. Sometimes the men had to lift the boats out of the water and carry them on land in order to avoid these sharp rocks.

As the party journeyed down the river, steep rock walls rose on either side. The tiny boats looked like dainty toys next to the towering walls of the canyons.

A few weeks into the journey, Major Powell spotted a waterfall and shouted, "Look out ahead!" but it was too late. One boat shot out over the falls, crashed into some rocks, and broke apart. The men inside the boat went flying into the water. Supplies were pitched into the rushing waters and carried away. Two of the men made their way to a small island downstream. One man clung to a rock in the river.

The men in the other boats saved the man who was hanging on to the rock. Then they went down the river to pick up the men stuck on the island. The next day, Powell and his men found the damaged boat. Powell examined the pitiful wreck of the boat. "Well, it could have been worse," said Powell. "Could be one of us here split in two instead! I'll be right glad when we are far away from these Disaster Falls!"

The men kept on going in the remaining three boats. Powell and his group would not give up.

A few weeks into the trip, the men started to become very weary. So, Powell decided to stop for a rest. In a nearby town, Powell and his men mailed letters home and picked up more food and supplies.

One of the men who went with Powell was named Frank Goodman. To Powell's surprise, Frank said to him, "I've had more excitement than a man deserves in a lifetime, and I'm leaving."

Now Frank had not expected to be coddled. However, he felt the risk was too great to go on. Sadly, Powell said good-bye. Now there were nine men left and three boats. The men were dedicated, however, and the journey continued.

Soon they reached the spot in the Green River where it joins up with the mighty Colorado River. It was even more dangerous to go on because the Colorado River was so fast. In spite of the danger, Powell marveled at the beauty of the canyons on either side of the river.

    The men stopped at the mouth of the Colorado River. They needed to fix their boats and to get rid of spoiled food. The journey ahead of them would be the toughest yet. Even so, they pushed onward.

    Rapid rushing water, called whitewater, closed in on the tiny boats as they moved quickly down the river. For miles the churning whitewater continued. Major Powell and his men had only their bravery and their skill to depend on. For weeks, the party journeyed in this manner. There was no time to stop and hunt as they had before. At times, the water was so rough that the men used ropes to pull the boats along the river from the shore.

The work was hard, and the men were exhausted, but they kept going. One day, the party came upon some extremely dangerous waterfalls. Three of the men decided not to go any farther because they felt the danger to be too great to carry on. Once again, Powell sadly said good-bye to his men. Now there were only six men left on the journey.

Even Major Powell was having doubts. He could not bear to give up, though, so they continued on. At times, the men and the boats rode the rapids. Other times, the men took their boats out of the water to avoid waterfalls.

Three days later, they finally reached the end of their journey. They had made it down the Colorado River, through the Grand Canyon, and to the mouth of the Virgin River in Arizona.

It was the end of August when the expedition finally ended. They had traveled more than one thousand miles (1,609 km) in less than one hundred days! Major Powell and his men helped many Americans understand the land of the West. Major Powell began to visit different cities and gave many speeches about the journey.

He wrote how he felt about the trip and the sights that he saw: "The Grand Canyon is a land of song. Mountains of music swell in the rivers, hills of music billow in the creeks, and meadows of music murmur in the rills that ripple over the rocks . . . All this is the music of waters."

Think Critically

1. Why do you think Powell wanted to make this trip down the Colorado River?

2. Read the last paragraph in the story again. What do you think Powell meant when he wrote those words?

3. If you could ask Major Powell a question, what would it be?

4. How did Powell and his men deal with the dangerous waterfalls?

5. What did Powell and his men do when one of the boats was destroyed by the rapids?

 Social Studies

Follow the Route Using a modern map, follow the route that Major Powell and his men took down the Colorado River. Find where the trip started and ended. Find the Grand Canyon. Name the states they would have traveled through.

 School-Home Connection Retell the story of John Powell's trip to a family member in your own words.

Word Count: 1,267